Inspiring Collective Biographies

AMAZING AMERICAN INVENTORS OF THE 20TH CENTURY

Laura S. Jeffrey

Enslow Publishers, Inc.
40 Industrial Road
Box 398
Berkeley Heights, NJ 07922
USA
http://www.enslow.com

Copyright © 2014 by Enslow Publishers, Inc.

Original edition published as *American Inventors of the 20th Century* in 1996.

Library of Congress Cataloging-in-Publication Data

Jeffrey, Laura S.
  Amazing American inventors of the 20th century / Laura S. Jeffrey.
      pages cm. — (Inspiring collective biographies)
   Summary: "Learn about these amazing inventors of the 20th century: William Lear, Philo Farnsworth, Beatrice Kenner, Gertrude Belle Elion, Gordon Gould, Charles Ginsburg, Robert Shurney, Jack Kilby, Stephanie Kwolek and Lonnie Johnson"— Provided by publisher.
   Includes index.
   ISBN 978-0-7660-4162-2
   1. Inventors—United States—Biography—Juvenile literature. 2. Inventors—United States—History—20th century. I. Title.
   T39.J439 2013
   609.2'273—dc23

                                                                  2012024611

Future editions:
Paperback ISBN: 978-1-4644-0245-6   EPUB ISBN: 978-1-4645-1159-2
Single-User PDF ISBN: 978-1-4646-1159-9   Multi-User PDF ISBN: 978-0-7660-5788-3

Printed in the United States of America.

042013 Lake Book Manufacturing, Inc., Melrose Park, IL

10 9 8 7 6 5 4 3 2 1

To Our Readers: We have done our best to make sure all Internet addresses in this book were active and appropriate when we went to press. However, the author and the publisher have no control over and assume no liability for the material available on those Internet sites or on other Web sites they may link to. Any comments or suggestions can be sent by e-mail to comments@enslow.com or to the address on the back cover.

✪ Enslow Publishers, Inc., is committed to printing our books on recycled paper. The paper in every book contains 10% to 30% post-consumer waste (PCW). The cover board on the outside of each book contains 100% PCW. Our goal is to do our part to help young people and the environment too!

Illustration Credits: AIP Emilio Segre Visual Archives, Hecht Collection, p. 52; AMPEX Corporation, pp. 54, 61; AP Images, pp. 18, 46; AP Images/John Bazemore, p. 94; Courtesy of GlaxoSmithKline, p. 43; Courtesy of Dupont, pp. 84, 90; Courtesy of Texas Instruments, pp. 74, 80; Farnsworth Archives, p. 24; Kansas State Historical Society, p. 8; NASA (National Aeronautics and Space Administration), pp. 64, 71; National Cancer Institute, p. 36; North Dakota Air National Guard photo by Senior Master Sgt. David Lipp, p. 13; Patricia Carter Ives Sluby Collection, p. 28; U.S. Patent Office, pp. 34, 100

Cover Illustration: Courtesy of Dupont

Contents

Preface 4

1 William Lear:
Inventor of the Impossible 9

2 Philo Farnsworth:
The Father of Television........................19

3 Beatrice Kenner: Making Life Easier ... 29

4 Gertrude Belle Elion: A Life Saver..........37

5 Gordon Gould: Receiving His Due..........47

6 Charles Ginsburg: A Team Leader 55

7 Robert Shurney:
A Struggle for Success........................... 65

8 Jack Kilby: The Might of a Tiny Chip ...75

9 Stephanie Kwolek: Strong as Kevlar ... 83

10 Lonnie Johnson: Ready, Aim, Soak! ... 93

Chapter Notes 102

Further Reading 108

Internet Addresses 110

Index...111

Preface

Alexander Graham Bell invented the telephone in 1876. In 1903, brothers Wilbur and Orville Wright perfected the airplane. Thomas Edison patented more than one thousand devices in the late nineteenth and early twentieth centuries.

So what have inventors done for us lately? Plenty. This book profiles ten American inventors chronologically by birth. Their names may not be familiar, but their innovations are. They created lasers, microchips, videotape recorders, and the Super Soaker® water gun, among other inventions.

These men and women are just a handful of the inventors who have helped make life in the twentieth century safer, more efficient, more entertaining, and even more exciting. Every year, the United States Patent and Trademark Office receives hundreds of thousands of patent applications. In 2011, 247,713 patents were granted. More than eight million patents have been issued since the Patent Office was established in 1790.[1]

A patent is legal protection issued to a person or company by the federal government. Products, designs, and processes can be patented, but ideas cannot. Patents for mechanical, electrical, and chemical innovations are called utility patents. Those given for ornamental devices are called design patents. Plant patents are given for plants that are reproduced asexually.

The life of a utility patent is twenty years. After that, unless a special act of Congress declares otherwise, anyone can use the idea without permission from or compensation to the original inventor.

To receive a patent, inventors first must determine whether their device truly is new. They can search through the files at the Patent Office in Arlington, Virginia, or they can hire a lawyer to search for them.

If the search does not turn up a similar idea, the next step is to submit a patent application. It should explain the invention with words and drawings. Models also were required when the government first started issuing patents, but that practice ended in 1870.

Examiners at the Patent Office study inventors' applications. They search through technical journals, textbooks, catalogs, and other publications to see if the idea already exists and has been documented. A patent is issued if the examiner determines that the invention truly is original as well as useful, and is not simply an obvious improvement to an existing device.

The patent process can take several months. Sometimes, it can even take years. In a very unusual case, Gordon Gould waited thirty years before receiving patents on the laser.

Patenting a device also can be expensive. Fees are required to hire lawyers and submit applications. Beatrice Kenner, one of the inventors profiled in this book, has five utility patents. Her first patent, which was issued in 1956, cost about $200. She estimated that a patent that was issued to her in 1987 cost ten times that amount.

Once a device is patented, it cannot be used without the inventor's permission. The inventor can sell the idea or can allow someone to manufacture the invention for a fee or royalty payment. This is the case with Lonnie Johnson's Super Soaker® water gun. A toy company manufactures and sells Johnson's invention. Johnson then receives a percentage of the profits for each gun that is sold.

Some of the inventors in this book created devices that changed the way we live, think, work, and explore. Gould's laser, for example, made new types of surgery possible. It also led to compact disc players and scanning devices at supermarket checkout counters. Jack Kilby's microchip is the "brains" of personal computers, pocket calculators, bank cards, digital watches, fax machines, video games, and smartphones. Robert Shurney's developments made space travel easier.

Other inventors helped to make our world safer and healthier. William Lear's imagination led to hundreds of devices that improved airplane travel. Stephanie Kwolek's Kevlar®, one of the strongest materials in the world, protects police officers from bullets. Gertrude Elion's discoveries led to drugs that help fight diseases such as leukemia, herpes, and malaria.

Some modern inventors enriched our culture. Philo Farnsworth invented the electronic television system. Charles Ginsburg created videotape recorders. Lonnie Johnson fired up his imagination to produce the Super Soaker, one of the world's most popular toys.

Still other inventors made life a little easier. Beatrice Kenner began inventing when she was six years old. Among her innovations are a back washer and a bathroom tissue holder.

The inventors profiled in this book are a diverse group. They are black and white, male and female. Some came from stable families, while others grew up in troubled homes. Many of these inventors raised families of their own, while others remained single. Some of them became very rich from their inventions, while others have received little or no money from their products.

These inventors also have some things in common, however. They all worked hard and refused to accept defeat. After facing tough questions, they focused on finding the answers. These ordinary yet very special Americans tapped into the power of their imaginations. Thanks to their struggles and triumphs, we all have benefited.

William Lear

1

William Lear

Inventor of the Impossible

William Powell Lear's success story is unusual. He came from a broken home, and his family did not have much money. His mother physically and verbally abused him.[1] Lear did not even finish high school.

Despite these obstacles, Lear persevered. With boundless energy and determination, he invented or improved hundreds of devices for airplanes. He also was the first person to make jet planes for business travel. Lear's other inventions include an automobile tape player and radio.

Lear formed several companies to make and produce his inventions. He was known for his willingness to work alongside his employees. Though he was a very demanding boss, many people found it exciting to work for such an inventive genius. Lear was called the Wonderful Wizard and Inventor of the Impossible.

"[Lear] had one speed: 100 percent straight forward," said Landis Carr, who worked with him. "He didn't have a slow, a pause, a stop, a rest, a reverse."[2]

William Powell Lear was born on June 26, 1902, in Hannibal, Missouri. He was the only child of Reuben Lear, a builder, and Gertrude Lear, a homemaker.

Lear said that his father "could work harder and lose more money than any man I ever knew." His mother, he added, was a "dominating woman with a violent temper."[3]

"We really had to scratch for money," Lear recalled. "All my early toys were discarded batteries and light bulbs and electric dry cells and bits of wire. I guess that got me interested in electronics."[4]

When Bill was very young, his parents separated, and he moved with his mother to Chicago, Illinois. Eventually, Gertrude Lear remarried.

As a youth, Bill loved to make things, but he did not receive much encouragement. He recalled:

> I would build a phonograph out of scrap materials. . . . I would get it to the point where, to finish it, I'd need a fifty-cent part which I could not improvise, borrow or steal. First, mother would scold me for wasting time on it. Then she would tear into me for not finishing it. When I would tell her I needed fifty cents . . . she would wallop me and say, "See, you not only waste time but you want to waste money!"[5]

By the time Bill was twelve, he had built a radio set with earphones. He also spent hours in the library. His favorite books were those by Horatio Alger. In Alger's books, poor boys became rich through hard work. These stories made Lear believe he could do anything as long as he was willing to try.

After completing eighth grade, Bill quit school and became an airplane mechanic. Sometimes he got rides on the planes he helped to fix.

In 1918, when Bill was sixteen, he ran away from home and hitchhiked to Denver, Colorado. There, he lied about his age and joined the United States Navy. World War I, which had started in 1914, was winding down.

Lear's first Navy assignment was in Chicago. He became a radio technician at Great Lakes Training Station. Six months later, with the war over, Lear left the Navy. He got a job as a telegraph operator. "As soon as I became the fastest operator they had, I quit," he said. "That's one of my cardinal rules of success. Quit a job the minute you master it. Get another job where you can learn something new."[6]

During the next ten years, Lear mastered and quit many jobs. He was a radio salesman in Chicago. Then he moved to Tulsa, Oklahoma, where he rebuilt a radio station owned by his grandmother's church.

Lear moved back to Chicago. He started his own business, building radios. His first invention was a coil for radios that produced a better sound.

In 1929, Lear began thinking about making a car radio. Other companies were making them, but they cost about $200. At the time, the car itself cost $600.[7] Within a year, Lear created a new and cheaper car radio. He also invented a radio remote control he called the Lazy Boy.

Lear earned a lot of money from these and other devices. With his earnings, he bought a biplane. After a lesson that lasted only about three hours, Lear made his first solo flight.

Lear learned that most pilots navigated by following railroad tracks through the countryside. In 1931, he started making a receiver called Radioaire. It gave off a series of electric clicks that led pilots to a beacon. They no longer had to look out the window for railroad tracks.

In January 1935, Lear unveiled a new direction finder called the Lear-O-Scope. This instrument used the government's low-frequency airwaves to help pilots keep track of their location over the ground.[8]

By the end of the 1930s, Lear had applied for fifteen patents. His company began making airplane receivers, transmitters, and direction finders. Lear often personally tested his inventions in his own plane.

In 1940, Lear filed for seventeen patents. Among his inventions were the Fastop clutch and the Learmatic Navigator. The clutch stopped the devices on planes that were operated by high-speed electric motors. The navigation device provided basic flight

The C-21 is a twin turbofan-engine aircraft used for cargo and passenger airlift. The aircraft is the military version of the Lear Jet 35A business jet.

information. It also helped pilots stay on course by tuning in to radio broadcasts. During World War II, every United States fighter, bomber, and cargo plane featured at least one piece of Lear equipment.

On January 5, 1942, Lear married Moya Olsen. She was the daughter of a famous comedian. Their son John was born in December 1942. Two years later, daughter Shanda was born. Moya and Bill's son David was born in 1949, and daughter Tina was born in 1954.

In 1944, Lear began experimenting on radio products for Air Force and Navy planes. He believed that fighter planes needed an autopilot system. This device made it possible for planes to fly automatically on a fixed course. It would enable fighter pilots to rest during long flights so they would be ready for combat.

Two years after his experiments began, Lear completed his autopilot system. In 1950, he was awarded the Collier Trophy for this invention. The trophy is given annually by the National Aeronautics Association "for the greatest achievement in aviation in America."[9]

During the Korean War, from 1950 to 1953, the United States military equipped its jet fighters with Lear's autopilot. America's first spy plane, the U-2, also was equipped with it. Throughout the 1950s, Lear continued to produce receivers, transmitters, automatic direction finders, and display instruments. These devices made flying much safer.

By the end of the 1950s, Lear was ready for a new challenge. In 1959, he sold his company and moved with his family to Geneva, Switzerland. There, he began designing an aircraft for business executives. Lear had never built an entire plane before, but he would not let that stop him.

Lear wanted to make a plane that weighed less than any other plane. A lighter plane would fly faster. It also would cost less to land and park, since fees were based on weight.

Lear moved to Wichita, Kansas, in the summer of 1962. There, he started a new company to build the plane. He and his staff worked all hours of the day and night. When they were finished, Lear's jet was lighter, faster, and less expensive than any other plane.

The Learjet had many new features. The doors opened out and up, rather than in. These new doors created an umbrella for passengers getting off. They also weighed less than traditional doors.[10]

Lear built the furnishings smaller than usual so the plane's cabin looked and felt roomier. He made the windows in the cockpit bigger so the pilots would not feel so closed-in. The electronics systems were improved as well.[11]

The Learjet's first flight was on October 8, 1963. "They said I would never build the plane," Lear said. "Well, I did. They said my plane would never fly. Well, it did. They say we won't succeed. Well, we will."[12]

The Learjet became the choice of celebrities. Actor Frank Sinatra, television personality Johnny Carson, politician Richard Nixon, singer Roger Miller, and television news reporters Howard K. Smith and Peter Jennings were among those who traveled by Learjet.[13] The Learjet also was the first American jet designed for business executives to be approved by the government.

Less than a year after his plane's first flight, Lear introduced a new car stereo tape player called the eight-track player. Previous players had only four tracks. With eight tracks, two hours' worth of music could be played. Lear's tape player also featured an endless tape cartridge. Drivers did not have to rewind or flip the tape while driving. This tape player became standard in automobiles.

Lear sold his company in 1967. He was sixty-five years old, but he was not ready to retire. He had a new project: a steam engine for cars and buses. It would be nonpolluting and would save fuel.

Lear moved to Stead, Nevada, to launch his new company. He spent millions of dollars developing his idea, but when he unveiled his steam engine in September 1970, it was a disappointment. The engine burned a lot of fuel. Lear dropped the project in 1974.

The inventor spent the last few years of his life working on a new type of plane. In 1978, he was diagnosed with leukemia, a cancer of the blood. Lear died on May 14, 1978, in Reno, Nevada, a month before his seventy-sixth birthday.

Two months after his death, Lear was named to the Aviation Hall of Fame. In 1993, he was named to the National Inventors Hall of Fame. He is remembered as an inventive genius.[14]

Lear himself was aware of the power of his imagination. One time, when Moya Lear expressed concerns about money, her husband replied: "Honey, you don't have to worry because they can't bankrupt my mind. There's an infinite supply of ideas there, and all I have to do is dip into it."[15]

Philo Farnsworth

2

Philo Farnsworth
The Father of Television

Philo Taylor Farnsworth is not a familiar name. Yet every day, millions of people are entertained and informed by his greatest invention. This bright, bold "boy wonder" was only a teenager when he developed his idea for television. At the time, scientists much older and more experienced than Farnsworth did not know how to send and receive clear pictures and words.[1]

Farnsworth received a patent for his electronic television system when he was twenty. He was called a genius.[2] Then he helped establish TV studios to broadcast programs. Today, thanks to Farnsworth, people all over the world turn on television sets to see dramas, comedies, weather reports, documentaries, and news shows.

Philo Taylor Farnsworth was born on August 19, 1906, in Beaver, Utah, to Louis and Serena Farnsworth. Philo had two sisters, Agnes and Laura, and two brothers, Carl and Lincoln.

Philo was shy but very smart. While other children his age played with wagons and tin soldiers, Philo tinkered with a toy generator and electric motor. He spent hours taking them apart and putting them back together. This was how he learned about mechanics and electronics.

When he was six years old, Philo told his parents that he wanted to be an inventor when he grew up. His mother was a little disappointed; she had hoped Philo would be a violinist.[3]

When Philo was twelve, his family moved to a ranch in Rigby, Idaho. The ranch had machines that made chores easier. Philo quickly learned how they worked. He also learned how to repair them.

One of Philo's least favorite chores was washing clothes with the manually operated washing machine.[4] Philo rigged up an electric motor drive that made the machine run much faster. After that, he had plenty of time to read books and magazines on science and chemistry, his favorite subjects. He also made scale models of automobile and airplane engines.

When Philo was a high school freshman, he was so advanced that he started attending the senior chemistry class. His teacher, Justin Tolman, tutored Philo before and after school so that he could learn even more.

Philo told Tolman that he was very interested in television experiments he had been reading about.[5] Scientists recently had discovered how to send sounds by changing them into electronic waves; that was how radio worked. Now they wanted to send pictures as well.

Many scientists thought mechanical systems, which required moving parts, would work for television. Philo believed mechanical systems could not work fast enough to send and receive clear pictures.[6] His idea was to televise images by changing pictures into electronic waves.

"I had known hundreds of boys before I met Philo," Tolman recalled years later. "But he was the one I knew was different. I had a feeling that I would never meet anyone like him again."[7]

In 1923, Philo's family moved to Provo, Utah. Philo, who was seventeen, began classes at Brigham Young University. He continued to work on his idea for electronic television. However, he did not have money to buy equipment to test his theories.

In 1925, Philo Farnsworth left college. His father died, and Farnsworth had to help support his family. The young man went to Salt Lake City and started a radio shop. However, it was not successful. Then, he tried working in the railroad yard, but he was not strong enough for the hard physical labor.[8] He also was anxious to turn his idea into a working television system.

"At that time, it was a daydream, a daydream only," Farnsworth recalled. "I had no facilities for doing research. I had no money to buy equipment."[9]

A newspaper job advertisement changed Farnsworth's life forever. George Everson was a fund-raiser from San Francisco, California. He was in town to raise money for Salt Lake City's community programs, and he needed helpers.

Farnsworth answered Everson's ad and was hired. It was not long before Farnsworth overcame his shyness. He told Everson about his idea for electronic television.

Everson introduced Farnsworth to a well-known scientist, Dr. Mott Smith. Dr. Smith was amazed that someone as young as Farnsworth had figured out such a complex problem.

"The boy's work is not only scientifically sound," Smith told Everson, "it is startlingly original and staggering in its implications."[10]

George Everson agreed to give money to Farnsworth. With that money, Farnsworth would be able to conduct experiments of his television system.

In 1926, Farnsworth moved to California. He was accompanied by Elma "Pem" Gardner. She had been his childhood sweetheart and was now his wife. They were married on May 27, 1926. On their wedding night, Farnsworth told his bride about his plans for the future:

You know, there's another woman in my life. . . . Her name is television. In order to have enough time together, I want you to work with me. We're going to be working right on the edge of discovery and it's going to be very exciting. I want you to be part of it.[11]

Philo and Elma Farnsworth settled into a four-room apartment. They turned the dining room into Farnsworth's laboratory. The eager inventor also set up a lab in an abandoned garage at 202 Green Street in San Francisco.

Farnsworth worked on his television system at all hours of the day and night. Elma helped her husband make the parts he needed for his experiments.

By the end of the year, Farnsworth had completed his design of an electronic television system. It could send and receive audio (sound) and video (picture) signals. This is how it worked:

Through a camera lens, an image was focused on a photo-sensitive tube. The tube was coated with a radioactive substance, which changed the image into electronic signals.

These electronic signals were sent as radio waves to the receiver set, where a picture tube changed the signals into tiny dots of light. These light signals were seen on the television screen as a duplication of the original picture.[12]

On January 7, 1927, Farnsworth applied for a patent for his television system. Vladimir K. Zworykin, a Russian immigrant working for the Radio Corporation of America (RCA), also applied

Philo Farnsworth's invention of the television has greatly affected life in America.

for a patent. RCA said Farnsworth's image-dissector tube, which was very important to his system, had already been invented by Zworykin.

The Patent Office held hearings to determine who had been the first to create the tube. The case was settled when Justin Tolman, Farnsworth's former chemistry teacher, testified. Tolman verified that Farnsworth had told him of the idea back in 1922.

Farnsworth received a patent for his television system on August 26, 1930. The patent included his developments for scanning, synchronizing, and contrasting. Scanning is breaking a television picture into electronic signals so they can be sent to the receiver set. Synchronizing is what happens when the transmitter and receiver operate at the same time for a steady image. Contrasting is making the picture signal stronger or weaker. Until the switch to digital TV in 2009, no television set could be built without using Farnsworth's creations.[13]

Farnsworth began demonstrating his television system to newspaper reporters in September 1928. Word of his accomplishments spread. Scientists from all over the world came to learn from Farnsworth and to work with him.

Good things were happening in Farnsworth's personal life as well. In 1930, Philo and Elma Farnsworth's first son, Philo, Jr., was born. The couple eventually had two other sons, Russell and Kent.

In 1931, Farnsworth and his workers moved to a laboratory in Philadelphia. That same year, Farnsworth helped Philco Radio Company set up a television studio. Philco received one of the first broadcast licenses. "Technicians in the Farnsworth Philadelphia laboratory have helped to make TV the dazzling dream of the decade," a radio reporter announced at the time.[14]

Three years later, Farnsworth demonstrated his television system at the Franklin Institute in Philadelphia. Eventually, he showed his system in countries all over the world.

In 1936, Farnsworth helped build a television studio and transmitter in Windmore, Pennsylvania. In 1938, he established the Farnsworth Television and Radio Corporation in Fort Wayne, Indiana.

World War II brought an end to television broadcast experiments. Instead, scientists worked on the war effort. Farnsworth and his family moved to Maine. He and his brothers formed a company to build wooden boxes to hold ammunition being shipped to American soldiers overseas. Farnsworth also invented black light, which is an invisible ultraviolet light. He created the first simple electronic microscope.

After the war, television broadcast experiments began again. By the 1950s, TV was common in American homes. The NBC, ABC, and CBS networks provided nightly programming.

Farnsworth Television and Radio Corporation was sold to International Telephone and Telegraph

(ITT) in 1948. Farnsworth worked at ITT on various projects until 1968, when he retired and returned to Salt Lake City. In the months before his death, he worked on nuclear experiments.

Philo Farnsworth died of a heart attack on March 11, 1971. He was sixty-four years old and had been married for forty-five years. The prolific inventor held more than three hundred United States and foreign patents.

In 1983, the United States Postal Service honored Farnsworth with a stamp bearing his portrait. In 1984, he was named to the National Inventors Hall of Fame. He also received the first medal of the Television Broadcasters Association, in 1944.

In 2011, about 97 percent of all American families owned at least one television set.[15] Philo Farnsworth's invention is used by millions of people, and it will be appreciated and enjoyed by generations to come.

Beatrice Kenner

Beatrice Kenner

Making Life Easier

Creativity runs in Mary Beatrice Davidson Kenner's family. Her mother was an amateur painter and writer. Her father and grandfather were inventors. Kenner herself earned five patents, more than any other African-American woman.[1]

Kenner never sold her inventions or made money from them. Instead, she invented for the sheer joy of creating. "I was never mechanically minded at making things," she said. "I was mechanically minded in thinking them up."[2]

Mary Beatrice Davidson was born on May 17, 1912, in Charlotte, North Carolina. She was the second of four children born to Sydney and Nellie Davidson.

Sydney Davidson was a preacher who thought up inventions in his spare time. His daughter recalled,

> He was very, very creative. . . . He had three patents. The first one I remember was a pants presser. It was part of a person's luggage. "Your pants would be pressing while they were packed for a trip."[3]

A New York company was interested in buying the rights to Sydney Davidson's invention. He was offered about $20,000, a huge sum of money in 1914. He turned down the offer, however. Davidson and his brother decided to try to make the presser and sell it themselves. "They manufactured one and sold it for fourteen dollars," Kenner said. "That was all they got out of it."[4]

When Beatrice was six years old, she had her first inventive idea: a self-oiling door hinge. "Every morning at about six my mother would leave the house by a squeaking back door," she recalled. "It always woke me up. So I said one day, 'Mom, don't you think someone could invent a self-oiling door hinge?'"[5]

Beatrice tried making the hinge herself. However, she was too inexperienced to complete the project:

> I [hurt] my hands trying to make something that, in my mind, would be good for the door. . . . After that I dropped it, but I never forgot it. Of course, what I had in mind was developed years and years ago. But I knew nothing about inventing. I just knew something should have been done for the door.[6]

Throughout her childhood, Beatrice thought up new gadgets and devices that would make life easier for her family. She often woke up in the middle of the night and wrote down her ideas so she would not forget them. She also made sketches and models of her creations.

"One idea my mother particularly liked was a sponge umbrella tip," Kenner said. The sponge was designed to stop water from dripping onto the floor after the umbrella had been used.[7]

Other inventions that Beatrice later came up with included a disposable ashtray holder that attached to the cigarette package. She also created a convertible top for the rumble seats of cars.

> If I can count back and remember, it would amount to around one hundred fifty-two articles I've created. . . . The patents I have, those were just things that I had some money right at that time to get a patent on. But I had other, very interesting, ideas.[8]

In 1924, Beatrice and her family moved to Washington, D.C. Beatrice became a regular visitor at the United States Patent and Trademark Office. She spent hours searching the records to find out if her ideas were original. Many of them were.

Beatrice graduated from Dunbar High School in 1931. Then she enrolled in Howard University in Washington D.C. After a year and a half, she left. Her family did not have enough money for her education.

Kenner continued to come up with ideas. However, she also needed to earn money to support herself and her family. At various times she had jobs as a baby-sitter and an elevator operator, among others.

When the United States entered World War II in 1941, Kenner found a job with the federal government. She worked for the Census Bureau, and later for the General Accounting Office.

Kenner also chaperoned younger women who attended dances at military bases in the Washington, D.C., area. In those days, single women were escorted on social occasions. One night when Kenner was chaperoning a dance, she met a soldier, and they fell in love. They married in 1945, but divorced five years later.

In 1951, Beatrice married James "Jabbo" Kenner, who also worked for the government. Previously, he had been a professional boxer. Their marriage lasted more than thirty years.

Five years after marrying James, Beatrice Kenner received her first patent, for a belt for sanitary napkins. She came up with the idea when she was eighteen years old. "One day I was contacted by a company that expressed an interest in marketing my idea," she said. "I was so jubilant. I saw houses, cars, and everything about to come my way."[9]

She added, "They sent a company representative, with a chauffeur, to my home on a Sunday morning to talk with me about it. Sorry to say, when they found out I was black, their interest dropped. The representative went back to New York and informed me the company was no longer interested."[10]

Kenner retired from her government work at the end of the 1950s—even she was unsure of the exact date—and then opened a flower shop. She operated the shop for more than twenty years.

After selling the flower shop, the Kenners moved first to McLean, Virginia, and then to Williamsburg, Virginia. The couple who were childless decided to become foster parents. Eventually, they took care of five boys and even adopted one of them. Who they named Woodrow.

Kenner received a third patent in 1976, for a tray that could be attached to a walker or a wheelchair. The inspiration for this idea was Kenner's sister, Mildred Austin Smith. Mildred had multiple sclerosis, a disease of the central nervous system that causes total paralysis. "After seeing her trying to get around on her walker, I thought it would be more convenient if she had a tray on it to help her carry things," Kenner said.[11]

Kenner's fourth patent was issued in 1982. It was for a bathroom tissue holder. A year later, Jabbo Kenner died.

Although she remained saddened by his death,[12] Kenner continued to invent. Her fifth patent, for a foam and terry cloth back washer, was issued in July 1987. The washer is mounted on the wall of a shower or bathtub. Bathers rub their backs against it to get clean.

In her eighties, Kenner continued to come up with new ideas. One of them was Nickless, a device to place on a car shoulder belt to prevent it from nicking the wearer's neck. "I'm short," Kenner said. "When I get in the car, that seat belt will nick my neck every time."[13]

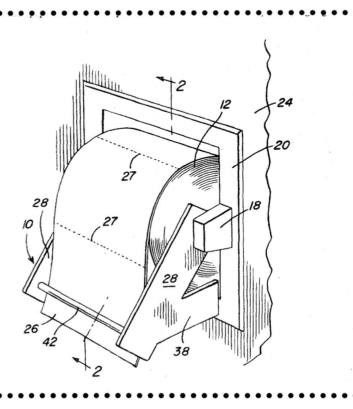

Patent drawing for one of Beatrice Kenner's inventions, a bathroom tissue holder.

Other ideas of Kenner's include a retractable hood to protect car windshields from snow and ice, and matches that stay out once they are used. She also came up with an idea of helium balloons to lower an airliner passenger cabin after a midair collision.

When she was not inventing, Kenner played the piano. She traveled to New York regularly to see Broadway shows, and she also enjoyed cooking.

Kenner hoped that young people, particularly African Americans, would catch the inventing bug. Out of about five million patents that had been granted by 1987, only two thousand were awarded to African-American inventors.[14]

Kenner even tried to interest young people in marketing her ideas. "I don't see black or white, but I do see that blacks are far behind in business concerns here," she said. "I plan to do what I can to help find a solution to the problem."[15]

Kenner passed away in 2006, but she remains an inspiration. For those who are interested in following in her footsteps, she offered this advice:

> Every person is born with a creative mind. Everyone has that ability. That doesn't make you an inventor. But if your feeling is very strong that you want to continue to create things, then you can do it. It's up to you.[16]

Gertrude Belle Elion

4

Gertrude Belle Elion

A Life Saver

Chemist Gertrude Belle Elion's inventions have saved thousands of lives. She and coworker George Hitchings created drugs to fight diseases such as leukemia, herpes, and malaria. They also discovered a drug to help patients survive after kidney transplants. Their research led to the discovery of AZT. This was the first drug to help sufferers of acquired immune deficiency syndrome (AIDS).

Elion and Hitchings shared a Nobel Prize for Medicine in 1988. Elion also was the first woman inducted into the National Inventors Hall of Fame. This honor surprised her, because researchers usually do not consider drugs to be inventions. "But I guess I invented new compounds," she said. "And then I had to discover what they were good for."[1]

Gertrude Belle Elion (called Trudy) was born on January 23, 1918, in New York City. Trudy's father, Robert Elion, was a dentist. He came to the United States from Lithuania when he was a child. Her mother, Bertha Elion, was a teenager when she emigrated from Russia.

Trudy's parents loved to read, and they passed on that love to their children.[2] Trudy learned to read before she started school. In the evenings, she and her younger brother, Herbert, listened to their father read aloud poems, biographies, and other books.

Trudy also was interested in science. Her childhood heroes were Louis Pasteur and Marie Curie. Pasteur was a French chemist who discovered that many diseases are caused by microorganisms. Curie, a Polish chemist who worked in France, won Nobel Prizes in physics and chemistry.

Trudy excelled in school. By the time she had finished junior high school, she had skipped two grades ahead of her classmates.

When Trudy was a teenager, her grandfather died from stomach cancer. She said:

> The suffering I witnessed during his last months made a great impression on me.... I decided that a worthwhile goal for my life would be to do something to help cure this terrible disease.... I decided I would major in chemistry in college, since that seemed to me to be the best road to the discovery of drugs that could accomplish my goal.[3]

Trudy graduated from Walton High School when she was just fifteen years old. The year was 1933, and America was in the midst of the Great Depression.

Like many other people, Trudy's father had lost a lot of money in the 1929 stock market crash. As a result, he did not have enough money to send his daughter to college. Trudy was able to get an education by enrolling in nearby Hunter College, which offered free tuition to any student who could meet the academic requirements.

Elion studied hard in school, graduating with honors in 1937. With her bachelor's degree in chemistry, she hoped to find a job in a research laboratory. However, women were discouraged from these traditionally male jobs. Elion was even told during one job interview that a woman would distract the male workers. "It surprises me to this day that I didn't get angry," she said. "I got very discouraged."[4]

Finally, Elion found work as a chemist for a pharmaceutical company. After working and saving money, she decided to go to graduate school. She enrolled at New York University in 1939, and discovered she was the only female in her class.

Elion lived with her parents while she attended graduate school. She also taught high school chemistry and physics. She graduated with a master's degree in chemistry in 1941.

By the end of 1941, America had entered World War II. So many men were needed in the military that a shortage of chemists arose in the United States. This shortage enabled women to obtain laboratory jobs. During the next three years, Elion worked as a chemist, first in a food laboratory, and then in a research laboratory.

In 1944, Elion met George Hitchings. He worked at Burroughs Wellcome, a pharmaceutical company in Tuckahoe, New York. Hitchings hired Elion as his research assistant.

Burroughs Wellcome hired workers to find drugs for incurable illnesses.[5] This was a difficult challenge, because drugs that could destroy a person's diseased cells usually destroyed the normal cells as well.

All living cells divide before they multiply. When they divide, they manufacture deoxyribonucleic acid, or DNA, which determines heredity. Elion learned how DNA formed in normal cells, and how it formed in abnormal cells. She realized that once she learned the differences, she could develop drugs that blocked the formation of DNA in abnormal cells while leaving the good cells alone.[6]

> If we can interfere with DNA synthesis in the abnormal cell without harming the normal cell, then we have a drug. . . . What you need is something that will hit one type of cell and not the others. Otherwise, you could just make a poison and kill all the cells.[7]

Elion spent long days performing experiments and monitoring the results. The days stretched into weeks, months, even years. She worked closely with Hitchings. In time, they developed a way of designing drugs to block the growth of bad cells.[8]

"The work became fascinating almost from the very beginning . . . ," she recalled.

> We were exploring new frontiers. . . . Each series of studies was like a mystery story in that we were constantly trying to deduce what the . . . results meant, with little biochemical information to help us.[9]

In the late 1940s, Elion developed a drug that slowed the development of leukemia cells. Leukemia is a cancer of the blood. It destroys body tissues and can lead to death.

Elion's drug was tried on some leukemia patients. At first, many seemed to have a complete recovery. Then they got sick again.

Elion conducted more experiments. In the early 1950s, she created another drug. It was called 6-mercaptopurine, or 6-MP. It helped children with leukemia live up to a year longer than they would without the drug.[10]

In 1953, the Food and Drug Administration approved 6-MP for the treatment of childhood leukemia. It became the standard treatment and is still used today, along with other drugs.

Elion's drug was a big breakthrough, but it was not perfect. Leukemia victims were living longer, but they were still dying from the disease.

Elion and Hitchings visited some of the patients taking 6-MP. When the drug did not work, "it gave us a terrible sinking feeling," Elion recalled.[11] She spent six more years trying to make 6-MP work better. Her research led to the discovery of a similar drug, azathioprine. It helped people survive after kidney transplants. Often, a body will reject a transplanted organ. Azathioprine can prevent this from happening.

In 1967, Elion was promoted to head of Burroughs Wellcome's Department of Experimental Therapy. Three years later, when the company moved from New York to North Carolina, Elion chose to move, too.

During the next ten years, Elion's research led to the development of acyclovir. This was the first drug used against herpes, a viral disease character- ized by sores on the body.

In 1983, at the age of sixty-five, Elion offi- cially retired, but she did not stop working. She lectured and attended scientific meetings all over the world. She also was a consultant to Burroughs Wellcome.

Five years after retirement, Elion and Hitchings were named Nobel Prize winners for their work thirty years earlier. They shared the award with British researcher James Black, who developed drugs for treating heart disease and ulcers, slow- healing sores on the surface of a mucous membrane, especially the membrane lining the stomach.

Gertrude Belle Elion performed many experiments in the laboratory of Burroughs Wellcome to develop drugs to help leukemia patients.

Elion said that winning the Nobel Prize was a complete surprise:

> People often ask whether this wasn't what I had been aiming for all my life. Nothing could be farther from the truth. . . . My rewards had already come in seeing children with leukemia survive, meeting patients with long-term kidney transplants, and watching [my drugs] save lives and reduce suffering.[12]

With the Nobel Prize came other honors. In 1991, Elion was named to the National Academy of Sciences, National Inventors Hall of Fame, and National Women's Hall of Fame. She received the National Medal of Science. She also held several honorary degrees and about forty-five patents.

In her seventies, Elion was busier than ever. She edited cancer journals, held seminars, and lectured around the world. She also worked with the World Health Organization (WHO), among other groups. "Everyone laughs when I say I'm retired, because I'm really doing just as much as before," she said.[13]

Elion also helped students at Duke University Medical Center with research projects. Working with young people was very important to her. "As I look about me and see young people shying away from science, I feel an almost missionary zeal to do something," she said.[14]

Elion also said she wanted to "spread the news . . . . that science is fun. I would like to see [students] experience the same excitement and fulfillment that I have had in my career."[15]

Elion lived until she was 81 years old. She never married or had children. She thought it would be too difficult to juggle a family and a career. However, that was only a minor regret in a long and rewarding life:

> I consider that I've made a reasonable contribution with my life, and I'm very happy about it. . . . Every time I give a talk . . . someone will come up to me and say, "I want you to know that I have had a kidney transplant for twenty years, thanks to your drug." Or, "My child who had leukemia when she was a child is graduating from college." And there really isn't anything that gives you better satisfaction than that.[16]

Gordon Gould, inventor of the laser beam, poses on November 7, 1977.
He finally got a patent for his invention after 18 years.

5

Gordon Gould

Receiving His Due

Gordon Gould knows the meaning of determination. He invented lasers in 1957. However, other people received credit for this important invention. Gould was accused of taking his ideas from other scientists. He fought for thirty years to receive patents.

Lasers are devices that produce very narrow, extremely hot beams of light. They can be used in many ways. For example, doctors use lasers instead of knives in eye surgery. Lasers also have been used to remove birthmarks, tattoos, and tooth decay.

Lasers also are used to drill tiny holes in aerosol cans and rubber baby-bottle nipples. Some lasers are so powerful that they can burn holes through diamonds and sheets of steel. They can be used to measure distance (even the distance to the moon), and can carry radio and television signals. They are also used to make and read CDs and DVDs.

Gould spent millions of dollars in his fight to be recognized as the laser inventor. "I knew from the beginning it was the most important thing I would ever get involved with," he said.[1]

Gordon Gould was born on July 17, 1920, in New York City. He was the oldest of three boys. His parents were Kenneth Gould, an editor and writer, and Helen Gould, a homemaker. "Even though my mother was not a technical person, she encouraged me to be one," Gould recalled.[2]

When Gordon was five years old, his mother gave him an Erector set. "At first, she would make things and I would take them apart," he said. "By the next year, I was making things and she was taking them apart."[3]

Gordon also fixed clocks for neighbors. Even before he was in high school, he knew he wanted to be an inventor. His heroes were Alexander Graham Bell and Thomas Edison. Bell invented the telephone. Edison invented the phonograph, the light bulb, and more than a thousand other things.

In 1941, Gould earned a bachelor's degree in physics from Union College in Schenectady, New York. In 1943, he received a master's degree in physics from Yale University, in New Haven, Connecticut.

With World War II raging, Gould spent the next two years working on the Manhattan Project. This was the top-secret plan to build an atomic bomb.

After World War II, Gould taught at the City College of New York. Then he began studying at Columbia University in New York, working toward a doctorate in physics.

While Gould studied for his doctorate, he worked as a research assistant in Columbia's radiation laboratory. One of his professors was Charles H. Townes. Townes had discovered a way to increase the power of microwaves, which are short electromagnetic waves. He called his advance *maser*, an acronym for Microwave Amplification by Stimulated Emission of Radiation. Townes's discovery led to new ways to communicate. It also improved radar and other sensing devices.[4] He applied for a patent in 1955.

The maser led Gould and other scientists to believe that if the power of microwaves could be amplified, or increased, the power of light could also be amplified as well. Light is another type of electromagnetic wave.

Light amplification intrigued Gould. He discussed the subject with Townes. In January 1957, he showed his professor a notebook of his ideas.

During a sleepless night in November 1957, Gould suddenly realized how to achieve amplification of light. He did not sleep the rest of the weekend. Instead, he filled a notebook with descriptions and sketches.[5]

"That notebook is absolutely incredible," said Peter Franken, a professor at the University of Arizona who saw the notebook years later. "It's as if God came down and whispered in Gordon's ear and said, 'Listen, buddy, this is what you're going to do.'"[6]

Gould's idea was to shine carefully controlled light rays on a material. The atoms in the material would absorb the light's energy. When the atoms had absorbed as much energy as they could, they would give off a powerful surge of light. Gould called his idea *laser*, or Light Amplification by Stimulated Emission of Radiation.

Gould asked a lawyer for advice on how to patent his invention. Gould thought he had to build a model to get a patent. Actually, inventors only need to provide enough information so that others can build the device.

Gould was very eager to develop his invention. He left Columbia University and went to work for Technical Research Group (TRG) in Melville, New York. TRG helped Gould file for a patent in 1959.

He was too late. A year earlier, Charles H. Townes and Arthur Schawlow had applied for a laser patent. Schawlow, a noted physicist, was Townes's brother-in-law. Townes and Schawlow, who received their patent in March 1960, came to be known as the fathers of the laser. In 1964, Townes won a Nobel Prize.

Other scientists also discovered how to amplify light. In March 1960, Theodore Maiman built the world's first working laser. He was working for Hughes Aircraft in California.

Gould's patent application was denied. He appealed to the Patent Office. Gould said Townes had gotten some of his ideas from reading Gould's notebook.

Townes denied it. He said he had been thinking about light amplification when he invented the maser.

Gould spent the next two decades fighting for laser patents. It took many years of court battles, judges' rulings, and legal appeals.

Gould was patient. Then again, in 1959 he never imagined how long it would take to get credit. "At no point did I expect it was going to take more than a couple of years to resolve whatever problem existed at a given moment," he said.[7]

Gould left Technical Research Group in 1967. He taught electrophysics at Brooklyn Polytechnic Institute from 1967 to 1974. Then he became vice president of Optelecom, a fiberoptical equipment company, in Gaithersburg, Maryland.

In 1977, the same year Townes and Schawlow's laser patent expired, Gould finally was awarded a basic laser patent. In 1979, he received a use patent, which covered lasers used for cutting, welding, and heating, among other things.

Gould retired from Optelecom in 1985. He received a final patent in November 1987 for gas-discharge lasers. These are used in operating rooms, at supermarket checkout counters, and in compact disc players. By 1994, Gould held patent rights to 90 percent of the lasers used and sold in the United States. They made him a very wealthy man. "The patents bring in a couple of million dollars a year," Gould said.[8]

In retirement, life was sweet for Gordon Gould. He had moved to Breckenridge, Colorado, with his

Some rough calculations on the feasibility of a LASER: Light Amplification by Stimulated Emission of Radiation.

conceive a tube terminated by optically flat

partially reflecting parallel mirrors. The mirrors might be silvered or multilayer interference reflectors. The latter are almost loss-less and may have an arbitrarily high reflectance depending on the number of layers. a practical achievement is 98% in the visible for a 7-layer reflector.① Flats with closer tolerance than 1/100 λ are not available so if a resonant system is desired, higher reflectance would not be useful. However, for a nonresonant system, the 99.9% reflectance which are possible might be useful.

Consider a plane standing wave in the tube. there is the effect of a closed cavity; since the wavelength is small the diffraction and hence the lateral loss is negligible.

① O.S. Heavens, "Optical Properties of Thin Solid Films" (Butterworths Scientific Publications. London. 1955). P. 220.

The first page of Gordon Gould's notebook, dated November 13, 1957, shows his conception of the laser.

wife, Marilyn. He and Marilyn had been together for more than twenty years when they married in July of 1992.[9]

Victory, however, was hard won. Gould spent millions of dollars fighting the Patent Office. He also battled companies that were making lasers without paying him royalties. Gould shared his laser royalties with investors.

The battles left Gould's reputation scarred. He was "discredited and abused for 20 years" as the man who copied his ideas for lasers from Townes, said Richard Samuel, Gould's lawyer. "Nothing could be further from the truth," Samuel added.[10]

Besides the three laser patents, Gould held twelve others. He was inducted into the National Inventors Hall of Fame in 1991, but he continued working on new projects. One of them "has to do with improving the processes of bridgework for teeth," Gould said. "My dentist challenged me to find a new way to do it."[11]

Gould's laser patents expired in 2004, and Gould died the next year, on September 16. The uses for lasers, however, remained seemingly limitless. Scientists predict that one day lasers will be used to help people communicate with distant star systems. They may enable airplanes and rockets to travel faster and cheaper. Lasers also might be used to provide the world with unlimited energy.[12] "I almost immediately saw the tremendous potential of this device." Gould said.[13]

Charles Ginsburg

6

Charles Ginsburg

A Team Leader

Charles Paulson Ginsburg transformed the television industry. He led a team of workers who invented the videotape recorder, or VTR. Until the microchip was developed, almost all television shows were taped with VTRs.

Before VTRs, television shows were broadcast live. TV producers could not edit out mistakes. They could not tape a show for viewing later. There were no reruns or instant replays.

VTRs also led to videocassette recorders, or VCRs. Every videotape and videocassette recorder uses Ginsburg's basic video patents.

His daughter Jane Ginsburg recalled:

> He was a brilliant man. . . . And he was an excellent team leader. Somebody would have invented the videotape eventually, but [my father] made it happen sooner. He knew how to motivate his workers. And he fought . . . to get them the space and money they needed for the project.[1]

Charles Paulson Ginsburg was born on July 27, 1920, in San Francisco, California. His parents, Oscar and Belle Ginsburg, called him Buster or Buzz. He preferred to be called Charlie.[2]

At the age of four, Charlie was diagnosed with Type I diabetes, a disease in which the body does not have enough of the hormone insulin, which is produced by the pancreas. Lack of insulin causes poor metabolism of carbohydrates, proteins, and fats. If diabetes goes untreated, it can lead to death. For the rest of his life, Charlie would need daily shots of insulin to make up for his body's lack of the hormone.

Because of his disease, Charlie was a sickly youth. His mother, Belle, spent a lot of time with him. She even pulled him to school in a red wagon so that he would not get too weak from walking.

Despite this, Charlie grew to love sports. He played hockey and tennis. He also began taking golf lessons at the age of eleven. Charlie's father was a doctor who had emigrated to the United States from Russia. One of Oscar's patients was a professional golfer. In exchange for free medical care, the golfer taught his sport to Charlie and his older sister, Marjorie. The game of golf would be a lifelong passion for Charlie. He played even after losing a leg later in life.

Charlie graduated from Lowell High School in 1937. Then, he entered the University of California at Berkeley. He planned to become a doctor, but soon discovered he preferred treating animals instead of people. So in 1939, he transferred to the University of California at Davis to study veterinary science.

College proved to be too expensive for Charlie, who was paying his own way. In 1940, he left school and worked in electronics jobs to earn money for his education.

After two years, Ginsburg had saved enough money to go back to school. He had enjoyed electronics so much that he decided to major in it in college. He enrolled in San Jose State College.

In 1944, Ginsburg married Louise Hammer. Eventually, they had five daughters. Jane was born in 1945, Marjorie in 1946, Nancy in 1947, and twins Peggy and Patty in 1949.

In 1948, Ginsburg graduated with degrees in engineering and math. The previous year, he started working as an engineer at radio station KQW in San Jose.

Ginsburg worked at KQW until 1951. One day, he received a telephone call from Alexander Poniatoff. Poniatoff was president of Ampex, a company in Redwood City, California, that made audiotape recorders for radio broadcasters and recording studios.

Ampex and other companies had been exploring the idea of tape-recording television images. Recording sound had proven to be fairly easy. However, there were problems with recording pictures and sound at the same time.

Video signals required recording speeds of up to 4.5 million cycles per second. Audio only required 30 cycles per second.

To tape the video with the audio, technicians had to play the tape at very fast speeds. Thousands of feet of tape were required to get only a few minutes of video playback. Also, the quality of the picture was poor.

Poniatoff wanted Ginsburg to be in charge of his company's videotape project. "I don't know why he called me," Ginsburg said. "My background was nothing spectacular. But he seemed to think I could do something with the project."[3] He also recalled,

> The opportunity to . . . work on the project was one that I jumped to accept. . . . It was a very exciting idea, the kind of challenge I wanted. After accepting the job, I was sworn to secrecy.[4]

In May 1952, Ginsburg began working on a videotape recorder. He was the leader of a team of workers that included Ray M. Dolby, a college student who worked at Ampex part-time. Later, Dolby would become famous for his breakthroughs in sound technology.

Ginsburg's team created a machine that scanned videotape in two directions at the same time. To pick up the video signals, the tape was scanned very quickly by the tape head. However, the actual speed of the tape was slow. This technique solved the problem of trying to record audio and video together.

Solving this problem required much trial and error. There also were many delays. At first, the VTR project was not considered very important at Ampex. It was postponed several times so that Ginsburg and his team could work on other projects. Ginsburg had to fight to get the resources he needed.

The first demonstration of Ginsburg's VTR was in October 1952. He showed Poniatoff a tape he had made from a cowboy movie. The resulting picture was "pretty fuzzy," Ginsburg recalled. "It was so bad that when it was over, the president of the company . . . said, 'Wonderful. Which was the cowboy and which was the horse?'"[5]

Ginsburg and his team continued to refine the VTR. By March 1953, they were ready to demonstrate another model. "While the picture was still not too good, the system had been much improved," Ginsburg said.[6]

More work delays followed the March demonstration. Finally, in February 1956, Charles Ginsburg and his team were ready to unveil another VTR model. They showed it to about thirty coworkers.

"The guests arrived, were seated . . . and the machine was then put in the playback mode," Ginsburg recalled. "It played back a program we had recorded an hour earlier."[7]

Ginsburg said:

> We then announced that we would record a sequence and immediately play it back. . . .We recorded for about two minutes, rewound and stopped the tape, and pushed the playback button. Completely silent up to this point, the entire group rose to its feet and shook the building with hand-clapping and shouting.[8]

Two months later, Ginsburg unveiled the VTR at the National Association of Radio and Television Broadcasters convention in Chicago. "The demonstrations were a bombshell in the industry," Ginsburg said. "Pandemonium broke loose and Ampex was flooded with orders."[9]

The VTR Ginsburg demonstrated in 1956 weighed about twelve hundred pounds. It was more than three feet high, and it was so wide that it could not pass through a standard doorway. Its size may not have been ideal, but its performance was. Finally, audio and video signals could be recorded together.

Ginsburg's VTR was used for the first time on November 30, 1956. CBS taped *Douglas Edwards and The News* when it was broadcast in New York. The program was seen three hours later on the West Coast. Soon, other networks also began using the machine.

In 1957, Ginsburg won an Emmy award for the VTR. These awards are given out annually for outstanding work in the television industry.

Ginsburg and his team had worked long hours at the office to make the VTR a success. "It was hard on [the family]," his daughter Jane recalled. "We would

Ginsburg (second from right) received an Emmy award in 1957 for his invention of the Video Tape Recorder.

have liked him to be around the house. When he wasn't working, he was playing golf."[10] Yet Jane also remembered a loving father who played math games at the dinner table. He taught his five daughters how to throw a football and swing a golf club.

In July 1959, Vice President Richard Nixon and Soviet leader Nikita Khrushchev held their now-famous Kitchen Debate. In this unplanned confrontation, the two leaders debated about the systems of capitalism and communism. The exchange was videotaped at an Ampex exhibit in the Soviet Union. The tape was then smuggled out of the Soviet Union by an Ampex worker. Later, it was seen by about seventy-two million Americans. This was the first time many viewers became aware of videotape.

While Ginsburg was enjoying success in the office, he had problems at home. He and Louise Ginsburg divorced in 1960. Two years later, he married Edna Perkins. They would stay together for thirty years.

In 1968, Ginsburg went to the doctor to get an ingrown toenail removed. His diabetes made the problem worse, though, and his toe became infected. Then the infection spread to his foot and leg. "It was one of those freakish things," Ginsburg said about two years after the amputation. "To save my life, they had to remove my leg.

"It's been a little hard to accept," he continued. "But then, it's just a fact of life and something I've got to live with."[11]

His daughter Jane recalled, "He wrote me, saying that he'd be back on the golf course in six weeks. And he was."[12]

Ginsburg was promoted to vice president of Ampex. He worked on VTR advances such as color and slow motion. In 1986, he retired. At his going-away party, he received an appropriate gift: a VCR.

During the first two years of his retirement, Ginsburg enjoyed golf and photography. He also wrote articles for technical publications. His health steadily became worse, however. In 1988, he suffered the first of several strokes.

Charles and Edna Ginsburg moved to Eugene, Oregon, in 1990. That same year, Ginsburg was named to the National Inventors Hall of Fame. He was credited with "one of the most significant technological advances to affect broadcasting and program production since the beginning of television itself."[13]

Ginsburg died of pneumonia on April 9, 1992. He was seventy-one years old. He is missed by his loved ones, but his accomplishments will long be remembered.

Jane Ginsburg said:

> Invention is not just one person working alone. . . Some inventions are team efforts. [My father] had the skills to persuade his workers to work long, long hours so they could accomplish their goals. So many of them told me that he was the best boss they ever had. They worshipped him.[14]

Robert Shurney

7

Robert Shurney

A Struggle for Success

Robert E. Shurney's life had never been easy. When he was a young boy, his mother died. He had to drop out of high school to help support his family. He did not earn a college diploma until he was forty years old. As an African American, he faced racial discrimination. Friends and foes alike told him he would never succeed.

Yet Shurney did succeed. He became a scientist for the National Aeronautics and Space Administration (NASA). His inventions made space travel much easier. "It had to be the will of God that kept me in line and led me in this direction," Shurney said. "Man alone could not have helped me. I was under-privileged, but I was determined early on."[1]

Robert E. Shurney was born on December 29, 1921, in Dublin, Georgia. He was the third of four children. His mother, Saint Clair Shurney, was a teacher. Robert's father, Vance Shurney, was a lumberman.

Saint Clair Shurney was a role model for her children. She wanted them to excel in everything they did. When she died, Robert, who was eight years old, was devastated.[2] He never found out how she died.

> My father decided it would be best if the kids were raised by someone else. So my older brother went to Florida to live with friends. The rest of us kids went to live with my grandparents in San Bernardino, California.[3]

Shurney did not see his father again for another twenty-five years. He did not feel abandoned, however. "I decided to look up rather than down," he said.[4]

Robert became interested in how things were put together. He was very good with his hands, and he built radios and a washhouse. The young boy also spent time at an auto shop owned by a family friend. This furthered his interest in mechanical devices and engineering.

Robert attended high school through the eleventh grade. Then, he dropped out to help support his family. He worked at odd jobs.

Eventually, Robert earned a high school diploma by passing an equivalency test. In the late 1930s, his grandparents sent him to Oakwood Junior

College in Huntsville, Alabama. "They wanted me to become a minister because they thought that I ran my mouth so much," he recalled. "But I did not want to become a minister."[5]

World War II interrupted Robert Shurney's college career. He was drafted into the United States Army in 1943, and he served as a medic for three years.

When the war ended, Shurney returned to Alabama, but he did not finish college. In 1946, he married Susie Flynt, whom he had met at Oakwood Junior College. The newlyweds lived in San Diego, California, for a year. Then they moved to Susie Shurney's hometown of Nashville, Tennessee.

Shurney worked as an engineer at a Nashville hospital for sixteen years. He took courses in electronics and pipe fitting to help him on the job. He also designed therapeutic equipment for the hospital's patients.

Meanwhile, his family was growing. Robert and Susie Shurney's first son, Darrell, was born in 1947. Girl and boy twins Glyndon and Glenn were born in 1948. Finally, two years later, in 1950, son Ronald was born.

Shurney became frustrated with his life. He wanted to make more of a contribution to society. He also saw white people with less experience get better promotions and raises at work:

> I had four kids to support . . . . I wanted to accomplish
> something, go somewhere and do something. But
> everybody told me I couldn't.[6]

Negative comments did not deter Shurney. Instead, they pushed him into action. He began thinking about getting a college degree. He discussed his idea with family and friends.

Early one cold morning, Shurney was at a friend's house fixing a broken pipe. As he worked, Shurney told his friend he was thinking about getting a college degree:

> He told me he didn't think I'd ever make as much
> [money] as my wife, who was a registered nurse. . . . That
> did it. I went down to Tennessee State University the very
> next day and took the entrance exam.[7]

"My friend motivated me by telling me I wouldn't be able to succeed," Shurney added. "I just pushed myself out there and made myself go on."[8]

Shurney began taking classes in 1956. After five years, he graduated with degrees in both physics and engineering. He worked full-time while going to college.

A few years before Shurney graduated, the United States had begun an ambitious space program. The National Aeronautics and Space Administration had been established in 1958. After John F. Kennedy was elected president in 1960, he announced that Americans soon would be exploring space.

The space program intrigued Shurney. He sent an application to NASA, but he was rejected. "They were hiring blacks only for menial tasks like house-keeping," Shurney recalled.[9]

Shurney contacted his sister-in-law. She worked with Martin Luther King, Jr., and his wife, Coretta Scott King, in their fight for equal rights for all Americans, regardless of race. Shurney's sister-in-law spoke with the Kings. They, in turn, talked to Attorney General Robert Kennedy, the president's brother. Kennedy wrote NASA a letter. He encouraged the organization to hire African Americans for professional positions.

After NASA received Kennedy's letter, Shurney was invited to the Marshall Space Flight Center in Huntsville, Alabama, for an interview. He was hired, and became a NASA research engineer in 1962.

Shurney spent the next twenty-eight years working for NASA. His first assignment was to work with weights and balances on the *Saturn V* rocket boosters. Soon he became involved with even more important tasks. In 1968, the *Apollo 8* crew made America's first manned space flight around the Moon. A year later, Neil Armstrong and Buzz Aldrin of the *Apollo 11* crew became the first people to walk on the Moon.

Future Apollo crews used the Lunar Rover, which also was known as the Moon buggy, to explore the Moon's surface. Shurney designed the tires that were used on the vehicle. His tires had metal chevrons, which provided greater traction.

They also were lightweight, so the vehicle would not be too heavy to transport into space.

Shurney designed the tires after studying the characteristics of lunar soil. The *Apollo 15* mission, in July 1971, was the first mission to use the Lunar Rover.

Much of Shurney's later work was done on *Skylab*. This manned scientific workshop was launched in 1973. It was used for six years to study Earth, the Sun, and the Moon.

Shurney designed toilets that were used aboard *Skylab*. He tested his invention in an aircraft that simulated the weightless environment of space. In fact, Shurney spent almost six hundred hours testing designs in weightlessness. This is more time than even the astronauts spent in weightless conditions.[10]

Shurney created a binding agent to mix with space food. It held the food together so it would not float away while astronauts were trying to eat. He also designed a container for the food.

Another of Shurney's accomplishments was the redesign of an instrument to determine the depth and density of lunar soil. This instrument also determined the vibrations of the lunar surface.

During his NASA career, Shurney helped design a solar shield and solar panel. The shield kept heat off the spacecraft, and the panel collected energy from the sun. The energy was used to run batteries, instruments, and equipment.

Robert Shurney designed the wheels for the Lunar Rover. Above, astronaut James B. Irwin works on the Lunar Rover during its first mission, *Apollo 15*.

Throughout his career, Shurney battled prejudice and misconceptions. He recalled many times when white workers assumed he was a janitor instead of a scientist. In fact, he often was the only African-American professional at the various meetings he attended.

Shurney received several awards from NASA for his innovations. However, he never pursued or received patents for them.

> You may have the ideas, the skills and the research, he said. But when you work for the government, [your ideas] belong to the government.[11]

In the mid-1980s, Shurney began working on a doctorate degree. He took occasional leaves from work and completed correspondence courses. In 1986, he received a doctorate in aeronautical engineering from Columbia Pacific University in California. He was sixty-five years old.

Shurney retired from NASA in 1990. He and his wife stayed in Huntsville, doing volunteer work in the community. Shurney also helped raise scholarship money for Oakwood Junior College. He died in Huntsville on November 25, 2007, at age eighty-six.

Shurney realized that becoming successful is particularly difficult for young people who are underprivileged. Yet he believed with encouragement and hard work, it can be done. As he said,

You don't have to do drugs. You don't have to stay out all night long. You don't have to prove anything to anybody but yourself. . . . Have some specific plan for your life. Strive to be better than what people might expect you to be.[12]

Jack Kilby

8

Jack Kilby

The Might of a Tiny Chip

Jack St. Clair Kilby was one of a few inventors whose ideas changed the world. He was the co-inventor of monolithic integrated circuits, or microchips. These small, thin squares are the "brains" of personal computers, pocket calculators, bank cards, digital watches, cell phones, video games, high-tech medical equipment, and fax machines. Computer systems for space and sea are other devices that depend on microchips.

The microchip was not Kilby's only important invention. In 1967, he and two coworkers created the first pocket calculator. It was based on the microchip that Kilby had invented nine years earlier.

Jack St. Clair Kilby was born on November 8, 1923, in Jefferson City, Missouri. He grew up in Great Bend, Kansas, with his father, Hubert Kilby; his mother, Vina Kilby; and his younger sister, Jane.

Jack's mother was a homemaker. His father was president of Kansas Power Company. During the summers, Jack went with his father on trips to other power companies. Jack was fascinated with his father's job. By the time he was in high school, the boy knew he wanted to be an engineer.[1]

In the fall of 1941, Kilby began studying electrical engineering at the University of Illinois. Four months later, the Japanese bombed Pearl Harbor, and America entered World War II. Kilby left school and joined the military. He worked in an army radio repair shop in India.

When World War II ended in 1945, Kilby returned to the University of Illinois. During one summer school session, he met Barbara Annegers. They were married in 1948, a year after Kilby graduated with a bachelor's degree in electrical engineering. Eventually, Jack and Barbara had two children. Daughter Ann was born in 1951; Janet Lee was born in 1954.

Kilby's first job after college was at Centralab, a division of Globe-Union Incorporated in Milwaukee, Wisconsin. In the evenings, Kilby attended graduate school. He received a master's degree in electrical engineering from the University of Wisconsin in 1950.

On the job, Kilby designed circuits for electronic equipment. These circuits contained thousands of parts. The parts were made of different materials to control and increase the flow of electricity. Then they were connected by wires to form electronic circuits.

Making the connections took a long time. Sometimes the wires came apart. This disrupted the flow of electricity and caused the device to break down.

Also, many electronic devices were huge because thousands of parts and connections needed to fit inside them. For example, some computers filled entire rooms, even buildings.

By the early 1950s, engineers realized that future devices would be limited by the cost, bulk, and lack of reliability of the electronic systems.[2] Kilby recalled:

> The numbers of parts and connections in some of these new circuits were just too big. . . . The simple fact was that you could not do everything that an engineer would want to do. It was pretty well accepted that this was the problem that had to be solved.[3]

In May 1958, Kilby left Centralab for a job at Texas Instruments in Dallas. A few months after he arrived, his coworkers went on a two-week summer vacation. Alone in the laboratory, Kilby began working on an idea he had about electronic circuits. He thought it might be possible for an entire circuit to be a single unit of silicon, which is a semiconductor. A semiconductor is a material that allows some electricity to pass through. This one unit would contain all the parts of an electronic circuit. It also would contain all the connections.

Kilby drew a picture of his idea. When his boss, Willis Adcock, returned from vacation, Kilby showed it to him. Adcock was not convinced that Kilby's idea would work, so Kilby built a model. On September 12, 1958, Kilby demonstrated his model. The first integrated circuit worked perfectly.[4]

Kilby and some of his coworkers built the first computer using integrated circuits in 1961. The computer was for the U.S. Air Force. It weighed ten ounces and had about six hundred parts. Without integrated circuits, it would have weighed four hundred eighty ounces (thirty pounds) and contained eight thousand five hundred parts.[5]

Meanwhile, other engineers were working on integrated circuits. One of them was Robert Noyce of Semiconductor Corporation in Mountain View, California. Although Kilby received a patent for the microchip in 1964, Noyce also applied for a patent. Noyce said he, not Kilby, was the first person to invent the microchip.

The patent fight lasted several years. Finally, Kilby and Noyce decided to share the honors. Kilby was the first to develop the idea for a microchip, and Noyce was credited with being the first to figure out how the parts would connect.

The microchip was not popular when it was first introduced. Most people thought it would be useful only for very powerful computers used by the military and in space. Patrick Haggerty, chairman of Texas Instruments, asked Kilby to create a product that would show Americans how microchips could be used around the house.

Haggerty wanted Kilby to invent a miniature calculator that would fit in the palm of a hand. It was to be much lighter, much smaller, and much cheaper than any calculating machine that had ever been thought of before.[6]

In 1967, Kilby used the microchip to create the world's first pocket-sized calculator. The calculator was very powerful, yet it measured only four inches by six inches and was less than two inches thick.[7]

The calculator began selling in 1972. It cost about $120. Kilby and his coworkers received a patent for it in 1974. Until then, most engineers relied on slide rules to compute numbers. The only calculators available were the size of large typewriters. They required thousands of parts and cost between $2,500 and $5,000.[8]

Twenty years later, more than 100 million pocket calculators were in use. Many cost as little as $5. "The calculator is as necessary in class as pen and paper," said David Wilson at the time.[9] He taught mechanical engineering at Massachusetts Institute of Technology.

Jack Kilby holding an integrated circuit.

"A problem that might have taken a week to do on a slide rule now can be done in about an hour on a calculator," added William C. Orthwein.[10] He was a mechanical engineering professor at Southern Illinois University.

Kilby left Texas Instruments in 1970 to be an independent inventor, saying,

> There's a certain amount of satisfaction in setting your own goals, in being free to do what you decide is important, and not pursue someone else's schedule. . . . The freedom, that's what interests me about this.[11]

That year, Kilby received the National Medal of Science from President Richard Nixon. He received the National Medal of Technology from President George Bush in 1990. Kilby won many other awards as well, including the 2000 Nobel Prize in physics "for his part in inventing the integrated circuit."[12] His first integrated circuit is on display at the Smithsonian Institution in Washington, D.C.

In 1978, Kilby became a professor of electrical engineering at Texas A&M University. In 1981, Barbara Kilby died. Jack and Barbara had been married thirty-three years.

In 1982, Kilby was inducted into the National Inventors Hall of Fame. The modest inventor's acceptance speech was only two words long: "Thank you." "He really didn't say a word during the whole thing," said Fred Ziesenheim, president of the Hall of Fame. "He just sat there like he was thinking about something. It looked like . . . he was sitting there working out his next invention."[13]

In 1984, Kilby left Texas A&M. He became a consultant for Texas Instruments and other companies. In his spare time, he read two or three newspapers daily, a dozen magazines a week, and all of the patents that were issued each year. "You read everything—that's part of the job," Kilby said. "You accumulate all this trivia, and you hope that someday maybe a millionth of it will be useful."[14]

Kilby also continued to tinker with inventions. He worked on ways to generate electrical power from sunlight.

Kilby died on June 20, 2005, after battling cancer. He had more than sixty patents, including patents for an electronic check writer and a paging system.

None of Kilby's other inventions have been as successful as the microchip. This tiny invention increased the reliability of electronic devices. At the same time, it reduced their size, weight, and cost. This made possible more complex, yet practical, devices.[15]

Robert M. White, president of the National Academy of Engineering, said,

> The development of the integrated circuit was the single most important event that helped usher in the Information Age. . . . Like the invention of the telephone, the light bulb or the automobile, the creation . . . of the integrated circuit has . . . changed our lives.[16]

9

Stephanie Kwolek
Strong as Kevlar

Do you think steel is strong? Kevlar® is stronger. This fiber is five times as strong as steel, yet it is lightweight and flexible. It is used in skis, golf clubs, tennis racquets, and bulletproof vests. In fact, thousands of police officers' lives have been saved because of Kevlar.

Kevlar's inventor, Stephanie Kwolek, also is strong. She had to be, to survive in a "man's world." During Kwolek's early life, few women were in the workforce. Women were expected to stay home and raise families. Those who did work usually chose traditional jobs, such as teaching and secretarial work. "That path is easier today," Kwolek said. "There are opportunities for women that did not

Stephanie Kwolek

exist when I started working. Then, if a woman spoke her mind, she quickly found herself out of a job."[1]

Stephanie Louise Kwolek was born on July 31, 1923, in New Kensington, Pennsylvania. Her father, John Kwolek, worked in a foundry. Her mother, Nellie Kwolek, was a homemaker.

Stephanie Kwolek recalled:

> I was never a tomboy. . . . I was a creative child. I spent a lot of time designing clothes for my dolls. I learned to sew when I was about six years old. But at the same time, my father had a scientific bent, and I spent a lot of time with him.[2]

Stephanie and her father explored the woods near their home, looking for different animals and plants. The young girl also visited family friends who lived on farmland with creeks and ponds. She enjoyed searching the water for fish, frogs, and insects.

When Stephanie was ten, her father died. Nellie Kwolek took a factory job to support Stephanie and her younger brother. The Kwolek children learned to be very independent.

In school, Stephanie's favorite subjects were mathematics and science. She decided to become a doctor. After she graduated from high school in 1942, she enrolled at the Carnegie Institute of Technology in Pittsburgh, Pennsylvania.

Part of the time, Kwolek lived at home and traveled to the campus by train. She also lived on campus for a period of time. After classes were over, she played bridge or attended science club meetings. She also worked during the summers.

Kwolek graduated with a bachelor's degree in chemistry in 1946. She said,

> I didn't have the money to continue my education, and there weren't the loans available that there are now. . . . So I decided to go to work to earn money for medical school.[3]

Kwolek's dream of becoming a doctor soon would be abandoned in favor of a career she found even more interesting and challenging. She became a chemist for E. I. du Pont de Nemours and Company. Kwolek first went to work in the company's offices in Buffalo, New York. Later, she was transferred to DuPont's offices in Wilmington, Delaware.

Nellie Kwolek was apprehensive because her only daughter was moving away from home, but Stephanie Kwolek had an independent streak. She also was excited about her job, even though she was one of the few female professionals in the company. During those days, many women, regardless of where they worked, quit once they got married or had children. They also left the workforce in frustration. Women were not paid as much as men in similar jobs, nor were they promoted as readily.

At DuPont, Kwolek joined other chemists who were working on creating synthetic fibers, which were less expensive and easier to care for than wool, cotton, and other natural fibers. Nylon, the first synthetic fiber, was produced commercially in 1939. It was followed by Orlon acrylic, Dacron polyester, and Lycra spandex. All of these fibers were DuPont registered trademarks.

Kwolek's job was to create new synthetic fibers that were even stronger and more durable than nylon. She worked with polymers, large molecules made up of many repeating, smaller, and simpler chemical units.

Some polymers can be melted. The resulting solution, called melt, is forced under pressure through the very tiny holes of a metal plate called a spinneret. When the melt is cooled, fibers are formed.

Kwolek and other chemists knew that some types of polymers, called aromatic polyamides, had stiff molecular chains and could make very strong high-performance fibers. However, it took such high temperatures to melt them that they decomposed.

Kwolek worked to find the proper solution in which to dissolve, instead of melt, the very stiff polymer. "It proved to be a time of great joy, and also of frustration," she said.[4]

One day in January 1965, Kwolek created a new solvent in which to dissolve the polymer. The solution then was forced through the spinneret holes. The resulting fiber was amazing. "It was stiffer than glass and very hard to cut even with scissors," Kwolek said. "But I didn't tell anyone at first. I had the experiment repeated and tested several times. Then I knew I had made a spectacular discovery."[5]

Initially, Kwolek's find was called Fiber B. Eventually, it was renamed Kevlar, which is a registered DuPont trademark. The name was chosen by a group of DuPont employees. "Kevlar is a very strong and stiff fiber," Kwolek said. "You think of it as a masculine fiber. And Kevlar is a masculine-sounding name."[6]

Kwolek received sixteen patents for her work. In 1980, she received the American Chemical Society Award for creative invention. The society cited her "research in chemistry which contributes to the material prosperity and happiness of people."[7]

Kwolek received many other awards from organizations and universities. However, she is quick to share the credit for her amazing invention. She said:

> I discovered the technology that served as the basis for the development of Kevlar. . . . When I made the initial discoveries, I was the only one working in this field. But then many people were assigned to work on the project. They also made significant contributions to the final commercial fiber.[8]

Once Kevlar was developed, Kwolek and her coworkers searched for ways to use it. This effort resulted in more than two hundred new applications. Its qualities were so unique, and its uses so wide-ranging, that it was called a miracle fiber.[9]

Kevlar first was used as a substitute for steel cord in tires. At speeds of one hundred miles per hour, tires made with steel ripped apart. The miracle fiber withstood high speeds. This quality was particularly important for tires on race cars and police vehicles. Also, tires made with Kwolek's innovation were puncture resistant.

One day, an official at the National Institute of Justice heard about Kevlar. He thought the fiber would work well in protective vests for law enforcement officers. At the time, the only vests available were military flak jackets or padded jackets. The military flak jackets were made of nylon and metal, and they were very heavy. The padded jackets, made of nylon, were very bulky. Jackets made of Kevlar were lighter than nylon, yet they were virtually bulletproof and knife resistant.

Vests made of Kevlar were distributed to police departments around the country. The first test of the garment came just before Christmas in 1975. Police officer Ray Johnson was standing in a checkout line at a Seattle, Washington, supermarket. He was off duty but in uniform.

A robber ran into the market, spotted Johnson, and pulled out a gun. Johnson was shot twice, and from only three feet away. His Kevlar vest stopped the bullets.

Other people began demanding Kevlar protection. Former President Gerald Ford had a Kevlar lining sewn into his raincoat after assassination attempts. Former first lady Nancy Reagan reportedly owned a slip made of Kevlar. Liquor store owners, shop keepers, bank tellers, and taxi drivers

For her important discovery of Kevlar®, Stephanie Kwolek received much recognition and many awards.

also began wearing Kevlar vests as protection against gun-toting criminals. Kevlar vests have saved the lives of more than three thousand law enforcement officers. Fireproof suits and military helmets made of Kevlar have also saved the lives of countless firefighters and soldiers.[10]

The uses for Kevlar expanded. It is featured in parachutes, suspension bridge cables, spacecraft, and linings for rocket engines, among other things. Kevlar cannot be a substitute for steel in buildings, though, because it bends easily under compression.[11]

Kwolek is proud of her work, and of her association with the DuPont Corporation, where so many inventions were made. Yet she believes people should not consider her invention superior to others. "Invention is invention," she said. "When the Patent Office issues a patent, it says officially, 'This is both original and practical.' An industrial invention, though it might be more complicated, doesn't necessarily show any more real ingenuity than a non-industrial one."[12]

Kwolek retired from DuPont in 1986 but continued to act as a consultant for the company. Her hobbies are gardening, reading, and sewing.

Sometimes, she speaks at schools in her area. She advises students to spend a lot of time reading and observing with an open mind. "I've noticed that creative people seem to notice things that other people just don't notice," Kwolek said.[13]

This inventive chemist never married or had children. "My mother would have liked for me to have married," Kwolek said. "But at the same time, she wanted me to get an education, and work at something that would be satisfying to me."[14] In that respect, Kwolek has more than fulfilled her mother's wishes.

10

Lonnie Johnson

Ready, Aim, Soak!

If you are one of the millions of people who own a Super Soaker, thank Lonnie G. Johnson. He invented this water gun, one of the world's most popular toys. Millions of Super Soakers have been sold in the United States since 1990, and millions more have been sold in other countries. Within twenty years, the invention had earned over $1 billion in sales.[1]

The Super Soaker's success allowed Johnson to quit his office job and become a full-time inventor. Yet the road to success was not always smooth. Johnson endured frustrations and financial problems. He also faced controversy. Some lawmakers called for a ban on Super Soakers after they were linked to violence. "The last thing I anticipated was a debate on gun control," Johnson said.[2]

Toy inventor Lonnie Johnson poses with his creation "The Super Soaker" outside his Marietta, Ga., office, Nov. 12, 1998.

Lonnie G. Johnson was born on October 6, 1949, in Mobile, Alabama. He was the third of six children. His father, David Johnson, was a civilian worker for the Air Force. His mother, Arline Johnson, was a nurse's aide.

When Lonnie was growing up, he took his toys apart to see how they worked. He also experimented with old jukeboxes, plastic piping, motors, and rocket fuel. His nickname was "The Professor".[3]

When Lonnie was a senior at Williamson High School, in Mobile, Alabama, he designed and built a four-and-a-half-foot robot. It won first place in an engineering contest at the University of Alabama. "He was something else," his mother recalled. "We were all amazed by him."[4]

Another time, rocket fuel that Lonnie had brought to school caught on fire. He was taken to the police station and accused of trying to blow up the school.[5]

Lonnie graduated from high school in 1968. Then he went to Tuskegee University in Tuskegee, Alabama, where he received a scholarship to study math. Johnson studied much of the time. "I can remember times when we'd be having parties," he said. "People would be dancing [to records] ... and I would be sitting there in the middle doing my calculus."[6] Johnson had made the record player for his dormitory room out of old jukebox parts.

While Johnson went to college, he participated in a co-op program, spending some semesters working at engineering firms to gain experience in his career field. He was working for Union Carbide in Florence, South Carolina, when he met Thelma Deas. They were married in 1972.

That same year, Johnson received a bachelor's degree in mechanical engineering. In 1975, he earned a master's degree in nuclear engineering from Tuskegee. Then he became an Air Force officer. He worked at the Air Force Weapons Laboratory in Albuquerque, New Mexico, as a nuclear safety officer.

Lonnie and Thelma Johnson's daughter, Aneka, was born in 1976. Three years later, Johnson left the Air Force for a job at the Jet Propulsion Laboratory in Altadena, California. He was a senior systems engineer.

In 1982, Johnson rejoined the Air Force. He worked on the military's spacecraft at Strategic Air Command Headquarters in Omaha, Nebraska. On the job, Johnson found ways to improve the memories of computers used in space. He also devised a new way for sailors to detect enemy submarines. In his spare time, he worked on his own inventions. His dream was to start a business.

Johnson created an instrument to measure distance digitally, and a soil moisture detector for farmers. He also started working on a new kind of heat pump. It used water instead of Freon, which can harm the environment.

One day in 1982, Johnson was in his bathroom tinkering with the heat pump. Suddenly, a stream of water shot across the bathroom. "I thought, 'Gee, this would make a neat water gun,'" Johnson recalled.[7] So he turned the heat pump into a toy water gun. It featured a pump to squeeze water from a tank.

Johnson let Aneka play with the toy. He also took it to office parties and picnics. However, it would be several years before others would be able to enjoy Johnson's invention.

In 1982, Lonnie and Thelma's second child, David, was born. Another son, Kenya, was born in 1985. That year, the Air Force sent Johnson to Edwards Air Force Base in California. He became a spacecraft engineer.

In 1987, Johnson again left the Air Force. This time he was ready to start his own business. Several companies were interested in buying his water gun and other inventions. Also, investors had promised him money to start his company. However, "Things didn't go as smoothly as I thought they would," Johnson said. "One by one, all of my projects fell through."[8]

The companies decided not to buy his inventions. More bad news came when his investors backed out of their financing deals. "I was left high and dry," Johnson said. "I found myself out of a job and living on savings. And I had a wife and three kids to support. Things were tough."[9]

To make ends meet, Johnson went back to work for the Jet Propulsion Laboratory. "All my little dreams just fell apart," Johnson said. "But I never stopped pushing and trying to be a full-time inventor. It was my campaign."[10]

In 1989, Johnson took his water gun to the Toy Fair. At this annual event in New York City, toy makers meet with inventors who have ideas to sell. There, Johnson met an executive from Larami, a toy company in Philadelphia, Pennsylvania. The executive was very excited about the water gun. He made a deal with Johnson. Larami would make and sell the water guns. Johnson then would receive money for each Super Soaker that was sold.

The Super Soaker arrived in toy stores in 1990. It was an immediate hit. "It was a real success story," said Gene Gillian, executive editor of *Playthings* magazine. "You hear so much about video games. You forget how good basic toys like . . . water guns can be."[11]

The fist Super Soakers came in several models. They included a pocket-sized version called the Super Soaker 20, and the Super Soaker 200. The 200 could shoot up to fifty feet.

Within two years, more than $47 million worth of Super Soakers had been sold. The Super Soaker was the most successful toy that Larami ever manufactured.[12]

With his invention's success, Johnson has become a wealthy man.

> I thought it was a good toy, a good idea. But I didn't know it would be like this. I knew it was better than anything else on the market. I didn't know people would go crazy over it.[13]

Johnson quit his job with the Jet Propulsion Laboratory in 1991. He moved with his wife and children to Smyrna, Georgia. Things seemed to be going well, but by June of 1992, controversy had erupted. Teenagers in Boston and New York were shot with real guns after Super Soaker battles. Police in several other cities reported that youths were filling the guns' water reservoirs with bleach and other harmful products.

These incidents led mayors and other officials to seek a ban on the Super Soaker. "These things should be taken off the market," said Clifford J. Willis, Sr., police chief of New Britain, Connecticut.[14]

Johnson responded:

> Kids also put rocks in snowballs, but you can't take snowballs away. . . . People will take anything and misuse it. It's not acceptable behavior, but they do it anyway. I think, actually, that the water gun is a good thing. That's what kids should be playing with, instead of real guns.[15]

The water guns now carry warnings not to shoot anyone in the face, and to use only tap water in the reservoir.

Lonnie and Thelma Johnson divorced in 1992. Professionally, however, Johnson was doing very well. After the Super Soaker, Johnson invented Jammin' Jets. These were planes propelled by water.

Johnson used some of the millions of dollars he earned from the Super Soaker to start several companies. At Johnson Research and Development

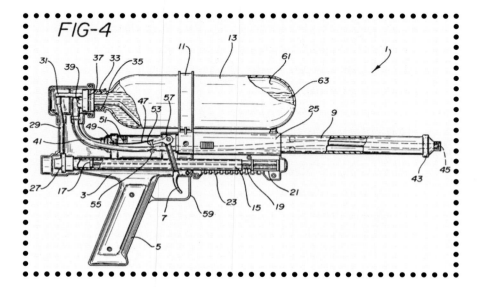

Patent drawing for the Super Soaker.

Company in Smyrna he developed toys and consumer products. His company was behind the NERF soft foam dart guns and Estes air rockets.

Johnson also works on high-tech products. His Johnson Tube is a refrigeration system that the National Aeronautics and Space Administration (NASA) considered using for cooling spacecraft. He also invented a device for detecting radon gas. One of his other companies, Excellatron Solid State, is developing a small but potent rechargeable battery. And Johnson Electro-Mechanical Systems (JEMS) developed the Johnson Thermoelectric Energy Converter, or JTEC (pronounced "jay-tek"). This invention uses heat energy to generate electricity, and Johnson claims it will be twice as efficient as solar panels.[16] Johnson believes JTEC could make solar power as affordable as coal.[17]

Lonnie Johnson has received over ninety patents, with more patents in the works.[18] He has little doubt that more will be coming his way. "Successful inventors are rare," Johnson said. However, "I anticipate that . . . I'll have even greater opportunities for success."[19]

Chapter Notes

Preface

1. United States Patent and Trademark Office, Arlington, Va.: "U.S. Patent Statistics Chart, Calendar Years 1963–2011," http://www.uspto.gov/web/offices/ac/ido/oeip/taf/us_stat.htm (accessed May 14, 2012).

Chapter 1. William Lear: Inventor of the Impossible

1. Sidney Shallet, "Aviation's Stormy Genius," *Saturday Evening Post*, October 13, 1956, p. 27.
2. Richard Rashke, *Stormy Genius: The Life of Aviation's Maverick Bill Lear* (New York: Houghton Mifflin, 1985), p. 170.
3. Shallet, p. 26.
4. David Shaw, "What Bill Lear Wants, Bill Lear Invents," *Esquire*, September 1969, p. 184.
5. Shallet, p. 27.
6. Shaw, p. 185.
7. Rashke, p. 40.
8. Ibid., p. 68.
9. Timothy J. Beals, *A History of the SLI Avionic Systems Corp., 1930–1987*, Smiths Industries, p. 6.
10. Rashke, pp. 239–240.
11. Ibid.
12. Ibid., p. 247.
13. Donald Porter, *Learjets* (Blue Ridge Summit, Pa.: Tab Books, 1990), p. 43.
14. "King Lear?" *Forbes*, March 1, 1977, p. 74.
15. Rashke, p. 140.

Chapter 2. Philo Farnsworth: The Father of Television

1. George Everson, review of "The Story of Television: The Life of Philo T. Farnsworth," *Newsweek*, March 28, 1949, p. 56.
2. Elliott Arnold, "His Vision Made Television," *Popular Science Monthly*, November 1940, pp. 74–76.
3. "Philo T. Farnsworth, Inventor of Electronic Television," Farnsworth Television & Radio Corporation, October 1939, pp. 1–20.

4. "Personalities in Science," *Scientific American*, February 1940, p. 69.

5. Farnsworth Television & Radio Corporation, pp. 1–20.

6. Ibid.

7. Mitchell Wilson, "The Strange Birth of Television," *Reader's Digest*, February 1953, pp. 19–22.

8. "Personalities in Science," p. 69.

9. Arnold, pp. 74–76.

10. Farnsworth Television & Radio Corporation, pp. 1–20.

11. *Television, Part 3: The Race for Television*, PBS, February 2, 1988.

12. Farnsworth Television & Radio Corporation, pp. 1–20.

13. "Farnsworth, Philo T.," provided by the National Inventors Hall of Fame, Pittsburgh, Pa.

14. *Television, Part 3: The Race for Television*.

15. Brian Stelter, "Ownership of TV Sets Falls in U.S.," The New York Times, May 3, 2011, http://www.nytimes.com/2011/05/03/business/media/03television.html (accessed May 14, 2012)

Chapter 3. Beatrice Kenner: Making Life Easier

1. Patricia Carter Sluby, "Black Women and Inventions," *Women's History Network News*, January 1993, p. 5.

2. Author's interview with Beatrice Kenner, June 25, 1994.

3. Ibid.

4. Bill Delany, "Inventive Mind: Kenner Always Has Something on the Back Burner," *Newport News Daily Press and Times-Herald*, January 13, 1988.

5. David Allen, "Inventor Tries to Make Life Easier," *Newport News Daily Press and Times-Herald*, December 8, 1982.

6. Ibid.

7. Allen.

8. Author's interview with Kenner.

9. Allen.

10. Author's interview with Kenner.

11. Ibid.

12. Author's interview with Kenner.

13. Ibid.

14. Patricia Carter Ives, *Creativity and Invention: The Genius of African-Americans and Women in the United States and Their Patents* (Virginia: Research Unlimited, 1987), p. 22.

15. Mike Lake, "A Passion to Invent Leads to Five Patents," *Virginia Gazette*, October 21, 1987.

16. Author's interview with Kenner.

Chapter 4. Gertrude Belle Elion: A Life saver

1. Marguerite Holloway, "A Profile: Gertrude Belle Elion", *Scientific American*, October 1991, p. 44.

2. Gertrude B. Elion, *The Quest for a Cure* (Research Triangle Park, N.C.: Wellcome Research Laboratories, 1993), p. 1.

3. Ibid., p. 2.

4. Holloway, p. 40.

5. Katherine Bouton, "The Nobel Pair: Mavericks of Medical Research in a Shared Quest," *The New York Times Magazine*, January 29, 1989.

6. Jean L. Marx, "The 1988 Nobel Prize for Physiology or Medicine: Three Researchers are Honored for Developing Drugs that Combat Some of Mankind's Most Common Diseases," *Science*, October 28, 1988, p. 516.

7. Don Colburn, "Pathway to the Prize: Gertrude Elion, From Unpaid Lab Assistant to Nobel Glory," *Washington Post Health Supplement*, October 25, 1988, p. 11.

8. Victoria Lofquist, *Science Lives*, KVOM Radio, 1991, University of Minnesota.

9. Gertrude B. Elion, "Gertrude B. Elion," *Les Prix Nobel (1988)* (Nobel Foundation, 1989), p. 4.

10. Elion, *The Quest for a Cure*, p. 8.

11. Ibid.

12. Ibid., p. 21.

13. Colburn, p. 10.

14. Elion, The *Quest for a Cure*, p. 22.

15. Ibid., p. 23.

16. Lofquist.

Chapter 5. Gordon Gould: Receiving His Due

1. Kerry Hannon, "Vindicated!" *Forbes*, December 14, 1987, p. 35.

2. Author's interview with Gordon Gould, June 21, 1994.

3. Ibid.

4. Eliot Marshall, "Gould Advances Inventor's Claim on the Laser," *Science*, April 23, 1982, p. 392.

5. Erik Larsen, "Patent Pending," *Inc.*, March 1989, p. 105.

6. Ibid.

7. Ibid.

8. Author's interview with Gould.

9. Ibid.

10. Marshall, p. 392.

11. Author's interview with Gould.

12. Brent Filson, *Exploring with Lasers* (New York: Julian Messner, 1984), p. 10.

13. Larsen, p. 107.

Chapter 6. Charles Ginsburg: A Team Leader

1. Author's interview with Jane Ginsburg, June 30, 1994.

2. Ibid.

3. From the personal papers of Charles P. Ginsburg.

4. Stanton Samuelson, "The Man Behind the First Fuzzy, 1,200-Pound VCR," *San Francisco Examiner*, February 26, 1986, p. A-1.

5. Ibid.

6. Ibid.

7. Charles P. Ginsburg, "The First VTR: A Historical Perspective", *Broadcast Engineering*, May 1981, p. 38.

8. Ibid.

9. Ibid., p. 40.

10. Author's interview with Jane Ginsburg.

11. "Three Courageous One-Legged Players," *Par*, April 1970, p. 41.

12. Author's interview with Jane Ginsburg.

13. "Obituaries: Charles Ginsburg, Video Recording Pioneer," *San Jose Mercury News*, April 19, 1992, p. 7B.

14. Author's interview with Jane Ginsburg.

Chapter 7. Robert Shurney: A Struggle for Success

1. Author's interview with Robert E. Shurney, July 11, 1994.

2. Ibid.

3. Ibid.

4. Ibid.

5. Notes for Fred Pullins's interview with Robert E. Shurney, July 1993, for *Oakwood Alumni Update Newsletter*.

6. Author's interview with Shurney.

7. Ibid.

8. Ibid.

9. Ibid.

10. Pullins's interview with Shurney.

11. Ivan Van Sertima, *Blacks in Science: Ancient and Modern* (New Brunswick, N.J.: Transaction Books, 1986), p. 249.

12. Author's interview with Shurney.

Chapter 8. Jack Kilby: The Might of a Tiny Chip

1. T. R. Reid, *The Chip: How Two Americans Invented the Microchip and Launched a Revolution* (New York: Simon and Schuster, 1984), p. 58.

2. Jack S. Kilby, "Invention of the Integrated Circuit," *IEEE Transactions on Electron Devices*, vol. 23, no. 7, July 1976, p. 648.

3. Reid, p. 22.

4. "Thirty Years at the Heart of Invention: The History of the Invention and Development of the Integrated Circuit at Texas Instruments," Texas Instruments, 1988, p. 4.

5. Sally L. Merryman, "Application for an Historical Marker Commemorating the Demonstration of the First Working Integrated Circuit," Texas Instruments Corporate Archives, February 19, 1988, p. 18.

6. Ibid., p. 133.

7. "Smithsonian Museum Accepts Historic Items from TI," Texas Instruments, December 4, 1975.

8. Irene Kim, "Handheld Calculators: Functions at the Fingertips," *Mechanical Engineering*, January 1990, p. 56.

9. Kim, p. 59.

10. Ibid.

11. Reid, p. 120.

12. "The Nobel Prize in Physics 2000: Zhores I. Alferov, Herbert Kroemer, Jack S. Kilby," http://www.nobelprize.org/nobel_prizes/physics/laureates/2000/index.html (Accessed April 29, 2012).

13. Reid, p. 195.

14. Ibid., p. 56.

15. Merryman, p. 17.

16. "Creators of Integrated Circuit Receive World's Top Engineering Award," The National Academy of Engineering, October 3, 1989, p. 3.

Chapter 9. Stephanie Kwolek: Strong as Kevlar

1. Ethlie Ann Vare and Greg Ptacek, *Mothers of Invention: From the Bra to the Bomb, Forgotten Women and Their Unforgettable Ideas* (New York: Quill William Morrow, 1987), p. 193.

2. Author's interview with Stephanie Kwolek, July 10, 1994.

3. Ibid.

4. DuPont thirty second television spot, DuPont External Affairs.

5. Lee Smith, "A Miracle in Search of a Market," *Fortune*, December 1, 1980, p. 94.

6. Author's interview with Kwolek.

7. Vare and Ptacek, p. 192.

8. Author's interview with Kwolek.

9. Smith, p. 92.

10. "Citation Conferring an Honorary Doctor of Science Degree on Stephanie Louise Kwolek," UDaily, May 31, 2008, http://www.webcitation.org/query?url=http%3A%2F%2Fwww.udel.edu%2FPR%2FUDaily%2F2008%2Fmay%2Fkwolek053108.html&date=2009-05-24

11. Smith, p. 94.

12. Anne L. MacDonald, *Feminine Ingenuity: Women and Invention in America* (New York: Ballantine Books, 1992), p. 375.

13. Author's interview with Kwolek.

14. Ibid.

Chapter 10. Lonnie Johnson: Ready, Aim, Soak

1. CNBC, "Meet Lonnie Johnson: He Made Millions Selling Water Guns," *How I Made My Millions*, The Life Files, September 22, 2010, http://www.thelifefiles.com/2010/09/22/meet-lonnie-johnson-he-made-millions-selling-water-guns/

2. "Hold Your Water," *People*, June 29, 1992, p. 89.

3. Jay Mathews, "Escaping the Office to Unlock Ideas," *Washington Post*, December 27, 1991.

4. Ibid.

5. Ibid.

6. Ibid.

7. Author's interview with Lonnie G. Johnson, June 1992.

8. Ibid.

9. Ibid.

10. Sheila M. Poole, "A Shot That Didn't Miss," *Atlanta Journal and Constitution*, February 1, 1992.

11. Ibid.

12. Author's interview with Larami Public Relations Office, June 1992.

13. Author's interview with Johnson.

14. "Hold Your Water," p. 89.

15. Author's interview with Johnson.

16. Logan Ward, "Shooting for the Sun," *The Atlantic*, November 2010, http://www.theatlantic.com/magazine/archive/2010/11/shooting-for-the-sun/8268/1/ (accessed May 23, 2012).

17. Ibid.

18. Johnson Research and Development, "Lonnie G. Johnson," http://www.johnsonrd.com/ie/lj/ljprofile.html (accessed May 23, 2012).

19. Poole.

Further Reading

Books about Inventors

Blashfield, Jean F. *Women Inventors 4: Sybilla Masters, Mary Beatrice Davidson Kenner and Mildred Davidson, Austin Smith, Stephanie Kwolek, Frances Gabe.* Minneapolis, Minn.: Capstone, 1996.

Casey, Susan. *Women Invent!: Two Centuries of Discoveries That Have Shaped Our World.* Chicago, Ill.: Chicago Review Press, 1997.

Challoner, Jack and Roger Bridgman. *Eyewitness: Electronics.* New York: Dorling Kindersley Publishing, Inc. 2000.

Cleveland, Donald B. *Seven Wonders of Communication.* Minneapolis, Minn.: Twenty-First Century Books, 2010.

Curley, Robert, ed. *The 100 Most Influential Inventors of All Time.* New York: Britannica Educational Pub. in association with Rosen Educational Services, 2010.

Henderson, Harry. *Communications and Broadcasting: From Wired Words to Wireless Web.* New York: Chelsea House Publishers, 2007.

Jones, Stanley, Jetty Kahn and Fred M. B. Amram. *African-American Inventors.* Mankato, Minn.: Capstone Press, 1996.

Klooster, John W. *Icons of Invention: The Makers of the Modern World from Gutenberg to Gates, Vol. 1.* Santa Barbara, Calif.: ABC-CLIO, 2000.

Krull, Kathleen. *The Boy Who Invented TV: The Story of Philo Farnsworth.* New York: Alfred A. Knopf, 2009.

Packard, Mary. *High-Tech Inventions.* New York: Children's Press, 2005.

Szurovy, Gezy. *Learjets.* Osceola, Wis.: Motorbooks International Publishers and Wholesalers, 1996.

Zach, Kim K. *Hidden From History: The Lives of Eight American Women Scientists.* Greensboro, N.C.: Avisson Press, 2002.

Books about Inventing

Casey, Susan. *Kids Inventing! A Handbook for Young Inventors.* John Wiley & Son Hoboken, NJ, 2005.

Erlbach, Arlene. *The Kids' Invention Book.* Minneapolis, MN: Lerner Publications Company, 1999.

Kassinger, Ruth. *Reinvent the Wheel: Make Classic Inventions, Discover Your Problem-Solving Genius, and Take the Inventor's Challenge.* New York: Wiley, 2001

St. George, Judith. *So You Want To Be An Inventor?* New York: Philomel Books, 2002.

Internet Addresses

To learn more about inventors, their lives and inventions, visit these websites:

Lemelson-MIT: *Inventor of the Week Archive*
<http://web.mit.edu/invent/i-archive.html>

The Great Idea Finder: *Invention Facts and Myths*
<http://www.ideafinder.com/history/of_inventions
.htm>

To learn more about becoming an inventor, check out these websites:

Inventnow.org
<http://www.inventnow.org/>

The Inventive Kids Blog
<http://www.inventivekids.com/>

The U.S. Patent and Trademark Office Kid's Pages
<http://www.uspto.gov/web/offices/ac/ahrpa/opa/
kids/index.html>

Index

A
acquired immune deficiency
    syndrome (AIDS), 37
Alger, Horatio, 11
Ampex, 57–62
Apollo crews, 69, 70, 71
AZT, 37

B
Bell, Alexander Graham, 4,
    48
Burroughs Wellcome, 40, 42

C
calculator, 6, 75, 79, 81
Collier Trophy, 14
Curie, Marie, 38

E
Edison, Thomas, 4, 48
E.I. du Pont de Nemours
    and Company, 86, 87,
    88, 91
Elion, Gertrude Belle, 6,
    36–45
Emmy Award, 60, 61

F
Farnsworth, Philo, 7, 18–27
Farnsworth Television and

Radio Corporation, 26,
    27

G
Ginsburg, Charles, 7, 54–63
Gould, Gordon, 5, 6, 46–53
Great Depression, 39

I
International Telephone and
    Telegraph, 27
Johnson, Lonnie, 6, 7,
    93–101
Johnson Research and
    Development Company,
    99–100

K
Kennedy, John, 68
Kennedy, Robert, 69
Kenner, Mary Beatrice
    Davidson, 5, 6, 28–35
Kevlar®, 83, 88–91
Khrushchev, Nikita, 61
Kilby, Jack, 6, 74–82
King, Martin Luther, Jr., 69
Kwolek, Stephanie, 6, 83–92

L
lasers, 4, 5, 6, 47, 48, 49–53

Lear, William, 6, 8–17
Learjet, 15–16
Lear-O-Scope, 12
leukemia, 6, 16, 37, 41, 44, 45

M
Maiman, Theodore, 50
Manhattan Project, 48
masers, 49, 51
monolithic integrated circuits, 75, 78–79, 82

N
National Aeronautics and Space Administration, 65, 68–72, 100
National Inventors Hall of Fame, 17, 27, 37, 44, 53, 63, 81
Nobel Prize, 37, 38, 42, 44, 50, 81
Nixon, Richard, 16, 61, 81

P
Pasteur, Louis, 38
Philco Radio Company, 26

R
Radio Corporation of America, 23, 25

S
Saturn V, 69
Schawlow, Arthur, 50, 51
Shurney, Robert, 6, 64–73
Skylab, 70
Super Soaker ®, 4, 6, 7, 93, 96–99, 101

T
Texas Instruments, 77, 79, 81, 82
Townes, Charles, 49, 50, 51

U
United States Patent and Trademark Office, 4, 31

V
videocassette recorder, 55
videotape recorder, 55, 58–62

W
World War II, 14, 26, 32, 40, 48, 49, 67, 76
Wright, Wilbur and Orville, 4